Fit...

C000088302

by Iain Gray

Lang**Syne**

PUBLISHING

WRITING *to* REMEMBER

Lang**Syne**

PUBLISHING

WRITING *to* REMEMBER

79 Main Street, Newtongrange,
Midlothian EH22 4NA
Tel: 0131 344 0414   Fax: 0845 075 6085
E-mail: info@lang-syne.co.uk
www.langsyneshop.co.uk

Design by Dorothy Meikle
Printed by Printwell Ltd
© Lang Syne Publishers Ltd 2016

ISBN 978-1-85217-255-8

Fitzpatrick

MOTTO:
The strong will yield to the strong
(or) Might is right
(or) The brave may yield to the brave
(or) Righteous and strong forever.

CREST:
A lion with a paw resting
on a dragon's head.

NAME variations include:
Mac Giolla Phádraig *(Gaelic)*
Fitzpatricks
Fityz-Patrick
Kilpatrick
MacGilpatrick
Shera
Sherar

Chapter one:
Origins of Irish surnames

**According to an old saying, there are two types of Irish –
those who actually are Irish and those who wish they were.**

This sentiment is only one example of the allure that the high romance and drama of the proud nation's history holds for thousands of people scattered across the world today.

It's a sad fact, however, that the vast majority of Irish surnames are found far beyond Irish shores, rather than on the Emerald Isle itself.

The population stood at around eight million souls in 1841, but today it stands at fewer than six million.

This is mainly a tragic consequence of the potato famine, also known as the Great Hunger, which devastated Ireland between 1845 and 1849.

The Irish peasantry had become almost wholly reliant for basic sustenance on the potato, first introduced from the Americas in the seventeenth century.

When the crop was hit by a blight, at least 800,000 people starved to death while an estimated two million others were forced to seek a new life far from their native shores – particularly in America, Canada, and Australia.

The effects of the potato blight continued until about 1851, by which time a firm pattern of emigration had become established.

Ireland's loss, however, was to the gain of the countries in which the immigrants settled, contributing enormously, as their descendants do today, to the well being of the nations in which their forefathers settled.

But those who were forced through dire circumstance to establish a new life in foreign parts never forgot their roots, or the proud heritage and traditions of the land that gave them birth.

Nor do their descendants.

It is a heritage that is inextricably bound up in the colourful variety of Irish names themselves – and the origin and history of these names forms an integral part of the vibrant drama that is the nation's history, one of both glorious fortune and tragic misfortune.

This history is well documented, and one of the most important and fascinating of the earliest sources are *The Annals of the Four Masters*, compiled between 1632 and 1636 by four friars at the Franciscan Monastery in County Donegal.

Compiled from earlier sources, and purporting to go back to the Biblical Deluge, much of the material takes in the mythological origins and history of Ireland and the Irish.

This includes tales of successive waves of invaders and settlers such as the Fomorians, the Partholonians, the Nemedians, the Fir Bolgs, the Tuatha De Danann, and the Laigain.

Of particular interest are the *Milesian Genealogies*,

because the majority of Irish clans today claim a descent from either Heremon, Ir, or Heber – three of the sons of Milesius, a king of what is now modern day Spain.

These sons invaded Ireland in the second millennium B.C, apparently in fulfilment of a mysterious prophecy received by their father.

This Milesian lineage is said to have ruled Ireland for nearly 3,000 years, until the island came under the sway of England's King Henry II in 1171 following what is known as the Cambro-Norman invasion.

This is an important date not only in Irish history in general, but for the effect the invasion subsequently had for Irish surnames.

'Cambro' comes from the Welsh, and 'Cambro-Norman' describes those Welsh knights of Norman origin who invaded Ireland.

But they were invaders who stayed, inter-marrying with the native Irish population and founding their own proud dynasties that bore Cambro-Norman names such as Archer, Barbour, Brannagh, Fitzgerald, Fitzgibbon, Fleming, Joyce, Plunkett, and Walsh – to name only a few.

These 'Cambro-Norman' surnames that still flourish throughout the world today form one of the three main categories in which Irish names can be placed – those of Gaelic-Irish, Cambro-Norman, and Anglo-Irish.

Previous to the Cambro-Norman invasion of the twelfth century, and throughout the earlier invasions and settlement of those wild bands of sea rovers known as the Vikings in the eighth and ninth centuries, the population of the island was relatively small, and it was normal for a person to be identified through the use of only a forename.

But as population gradually increased and there were many more people with the same forename, surnames were adopted to distinguish one person, or one community, from another.

Individuals identified themselves with their own particular tribe, or 'tuath', and this tribe – that also became known as a clann, or clan – took its name from some distinguished ancestor who had founded the clan.

The Gaelic-Irish form of the name Kelly, for example, is Ó Ceallaigh, or O'Kelly, indicating descent from an original 'Ceallaigh', with the 'O' denoting 'grandson of.' The name was later anglicised to Kelly.

The prefix 'Mac' or 'Mc', meanwhile, as with the clans of the Scottish Highlands, denotes 'son of.'

Although the Irish clans had much in common with their Scottish counterparts, one important difference lies in what are known as 'septs', or branches, of the clan.

Septs of Scottish clans were groups who often bore an entirely different name from the clan name but were under the clan's protection.

In Ireland, septs were groups that shared the same name and who could be found scattered throughout the four provinces of Ulster, Leinster, Munster, and Connacht.

The 'golden age' of the Gaelic-Irish clans, infused as their veins were with the blood of Celts, pre-dates the Viking invasions of the eighth and ninth centuries and the Norman invasion of the twelfth century, and the sacred heart of the country was the Hill of Tara, near the River Boyne, in County Meath.

Known in Gaelic as 'Teamhar na Rí', or Hill of Kings, it was the royal seat of the 'Ard Rí Éireann', or High King of Ireland, to whom the petty kings, or chieftains, from the island's provinces were ultimately subordinate.

It was on the Hill of Tara, beside a stone pillar known as the Irish 'Lia Fáil', or Stone of Destiny, that the High Kings were inaugurated and, according to legend, this stone would emit a piercing screech that could be heard all over Ireland when touched by the hand of the rightful king.

The Hill of Tara is today one of the island's main tourist attractions.

Opposition to English rule over Ireland, established in the wake of the Cambro-Norman invasion, broke out frequently and the harsh solution adopted by the powerful forces of the Crown was to forcibly evict the native Irish from their lands.

These lands were then granted to Protestant colonists, or 'planters', from Britain.

Many of these colonists, ironically, came from Scotland and were the descendants of the original 'Scotti', or 'Scots', who gave their name to Scotland after migrating there in the fifth century A.D., from the north of Ireland.

Colonisation entailed harsh penal laws being imposed on the majority of the native Irish population, stripping them practically of all of their rights.

The Crown's main bastion in Ireland was Dublin and its environs, known as the Pale, and it was the dispossessed peasantry who lived outside this Pale, desperately striving to eke out a meagre living.

It was this that gave rise to the modern-day expression of someone or something being 'beyond the pale'.

Attempts were made to stamp out all aspects of the ancient Gaelic-Irish culture, to the extent that even to bear a Gaelic-Irish name was to invite discrimination.

This is why many Gaelic-Irish names were anglicised with, for example, and noted above, Ó Ceallaigh, or O'Kelly, being anglicised to Kelly.

Succeeding centuries have seen strong revivals of Gaelic-Irish consciousness, however, and this has led to many families reverting back to the original form of their name, while the language itself is frequently found on the fluent tongues of an estimated 90,000 to 145,000 of the island's population.

Ireland's turbulent history of religious and political strife is one that lasted well into the twentieth century, a landmark century that saw the partition of the island into the twenty-six counties of the independent Republic of

Ireland, or Eire, and the six counties of Northern Ireland, or Ulster.

Dublin, originally founded by Vikings, is now a vibrant and truly cosmopolitan city while the proud city of Belfast is one of the jewels in the crown of Ulster.

It was Saint Patrick who first brought the light of Christianity to Ireland in the fifth century A.D.

Interpretations of this Christian message have varied over the centuries, often leading to bitter sectarian conflict – but the many intricately sculpted Celtic Crosses found all over the island are symbolic of a unity that crosses the sectarian divide.

It is an image that fuses the 'old gods' of the Celts with Christianity.

All the signs from the early years of this new millennium indicate that sectarian strife may soon become a thing of the past – with the Irish and their many kinsfolk across the world, be they Protestant or Catholic, finding common purpose in the rich tapestry of their shared heritage.

Chapter two:

The devotees of St. Patrick

The Fitzpatrick surname is truly unique in that, contrary to common belief, it is the only name with a 'fitz' prefix that is not of Norman origin, such as, for example, Fitzgerald and Fitzstephen.

The Fitzpatricks, in fact, were a truly native Irish clan, with the original Gaelic form of the name being Mac Giolla Phádraig.

The clan traces a descent from one of the sons of Milesius, a king of what is now modern day Spain, and who had planned to invade Ireland in fulfilment of a mysterious Druidic prophecy.

Milesius died before he could launch his invasion across the sea to Ireland, but eight sons who included Amergin, Hebor, Ir, and Heremon undertook the task.

Five sons, including Ir, were killed in battle against the Tuatha De Danann shortly after battling their way from the shoreline to the soil of Ireland.

This was soil, however, that Ir's offspring and the offspring of his brothers Heber and Heremon were destined to hold for centuries as warrior kings.

According to the Milesian genealogies, Heremon and Heber began to rule the land they had conquered from about 1699 B.C.

The Fitzpatricks trace a descent back to Heremon, who killed both Amergin and Heber in quarrels over territory.

Towards the end of the second century A.D. Heremon's descendant Aengus Osrith had founded the kingdom of Ossory, in the ancient province of Leinster.

It was a descendant of his, Giolla Phádraig, king of Ossory from 976 A.D. to 996 A.D. who gave his name to what became the Fitzpatricks of today – with Mac Giolla Phádraig denoting 'son of Phádraig.'

'Giolla Phadraig', in turn, denotes 'devotee of St. Patrick' and, accordingly, it is with this Irish saint that the proud heritage of the Fitzpatricks of today is closely bound.

The life and times of St. Patrick, who, along with Brigid of Kildare and Columba is recognised as an Irish patron saint, were truly thrilling and made of the stuff of legend.

He is thought to have been born about 373 A.D. to a Romano-British family in the area of present day Milford Haven, in Wales.

It was only a short sea journey from the east coast of Ireland to Wales, and raids on its coastline were commonplace by Irish chieftains and their kinsfolk in search of rich booty and plunder.

When he was aged about 16, the future saint was captured in one of these raids by none other than the legendary Irish warrior king Niall of the Nine Hostages and endured six years as a slave in Ireland before escaping and returning to his family.

Undaunted by his six years of slavery, he returned to Ireland – but this time in the form of a missionary to spread the light of Christianity throughout the island.

Miraculous powers were ascribed to the saint, known in Gaelic as Naomh Pádraig, not the least of which was the power to drive all serpents from Ireland.

In common with all legends this is rooted in a degree of rather intriguing historical truth.

The main opponents of what was then the 'new' religion of Christianity were the Druids.

One of their symbols was the serpent, and the legend that refers to St. Patrick driving out the serpents is believed to refer to him driving out the Druids.

One reason, meanwhile, why the clover known as the shamrock holds such significance to the Irish is that in order to explain the Christian concept of the Trinity of 'Father, Son, and Holy Ghost', St. Patrick used the three-leaved shamrock.

The date of his death remains uncertain, some sources asserting it was in 461 A.D.

His death date, or feast day, however, is celebrated annually worldwide on March 17, known as St. Patrick's Day.

The Mac Giolla Phádraigs flourished for centuries in Ossory, with the Chief of the Clan known as the Lord of Upper Ossory – but although they could not have known it at the time, what would prove to be the death knell of their ancient way of life and that of other native Irish clans would be sounded in the late twelfth century.

This was in the form of invasion – an invasion, ironically, that was launched from the same coastline from which St. Patrick had been taken centuries earlier by Niall of the Nine Hostages and from where he later launched his evangelising mission to the island.

Twelfth century Ireland was far from being a unified nation, split up as it was into territories ruled over by squabbling chieftains such as the Lords of Upper Ossory, who ruled as kings in their own right – and this inter-clan rivalry worked to the advantage of the invaders.

In a series of bloody conflicts one chieftain, or king, would occasionally gain the upper hand over his rivals, and by 1156 the most powerful was Muirchertach MacLochlainn, king of the powerful O'Neills.

He was opposed by the equally powerful Rory O'Connor, king of the province of Connacht, but he increased his power and influence by allying himself with Dermot MacMurrough, king of Leinster – who had already crushed expansionist ambitions by the Mac Giolla Phádraig Lord of Upper Ossory.

MacLochlainn and MacMurrough were aware that the main key to the kingdom of Ireland was the thriving trading port of Dublin that had been established by invading Vikings, or Ostmen, in 852 A.D. Dublin was taken by the combined forces of the Leinster and Connacht kings, but when MacLochlainn died the Dubliners rose up in revolt and overthrew the unpopular MacMurrough.

A triumphant Rory O'Connor entered Dublin and was later inaugurated as Ard Rí, or High King, but MacMurrough refused to accept defeat.

He appealed for help from England's Henry II in unseating O'Connor, an act that was to radically affect the future course of Ireland's fortunes.

The English monarch agreed to help MacMurrough, but distanced himself from direct action by delegating his Norman subjects in Wales with the task.

These ambitious and battle-hardened barons and knights had first settled in Wales following the Norman Conquest of England in 1066 and, with an eye on rich booty, plunder, and lands, were only too eager to obey their sovereign's wishes and furnish aid to MacMurrough.

MacMurrough crossed the Irish Sea to Bristol, where he rallied powerful barons such as Robert Fitzstephen and Maurice Fitzgerald to his cause, along with Gilbert de Clare, Earl of Pembroke.

The mighty Norman war machine soon moved into action, and so fierce and disciplined was their onslaught on the forces of Rory O'Connor and his allies that by 1171 they had re-captured Dublin, in the name of MacMurrough, and other strategically important territories.

It was now that a nervous Henry II began to take cold feet over the venture, realising that he may have created a rival in the form of a separate Norman kingdom in Ireland.

Accordingly, he landed on the island, near Waterford, at

the head of a large army in October of 1171 with the aim of curbing the power of his Cambro-Norman barons.

Protracted war between the king and his barons was averted, however, when they submitted to the royal will, promising homage and allegiance in return for holding the territories they had conquered in the king's name.

Henry also received the reluctant submission and homage of many of the Irish chieftains.

English dominion over Ireland was ratified through the Treaty of Windsor of 1175, under the terms of which Rory O'Connor, for example, was allowed to rule territory unoccupied by the Normans in the role of a vassal of the king.

The English Crown's grip on Ireland tightened as waves of other Norman settlers descended on the island, at the expense of native Irish families such as the Mac Giolla Phádraigs, who lost much of their power to mighty Norman magnates such as the Ormond Butlers.

In bid to preserve what power and territories they had, many native Irish families had no option but to reluctantly seek some sort of accommodation with the English Crown –not least the Mac Giolla Phádraigs.

In 1541 England's Henry VIII created Brian Mac Giolla Phádraig Lord Baron of Upper Ossory.

But there was a price to be paid – he had to change his Gaelic surname to one more 'acceptable' to English ears, and the one chosen was Fitzpatrick.

Chapter three:

Death of the Gaelic order

Maintaining an accommodation with the powerful forces of the English Crown was never an easy matter, with families such as the Fitzpatricks having to carefully walk a tightrope between survival and destruction.

Matters came to a bloody head in 1641 when Catholic landowners rebelled against the Crown's policy of settling, or 'planting' loyal Protestants on Irish land.

This policy had started during the reign from 1491 to 1547 of Henry VIII, whose Reformation effectively outlawed the established Roman Catholic faith throughout his dominions.

This settlement of loyal Protestants in Ireland continued throughout the subsequent reigns of Elizabeth I, James I (James VI of Scotland), and Charles I.

In an insurrection that exploded in 1641, at least 2,000 Protestant settlers were massacred at the hands of Catholic landowners and their native Irish peasantry.

Thousands more were stripped of their belongings and driven from their lands to seek refuge where they could.

Terrible as the atrocities were against the Protestant settlers, subsequent accounts became greatly exaggerated, serving to fuel a burning desire on the part of Protestants for revenge against the rebels.

Tragically for Ireland, this revenge became directed not only against the rebels, but native Irish Catholics such as the Fitzpatricks in general.

The English Civil War intervened to prevent immediate action against the rebels, but following the execution of Charles I in 1649 and the consolidation of the power of England's fanatically Protestant Oliver Cromwell, the time was ripe for revenge.

The Lord Protector, as he was named, descended on Ireland at the head of a 20,000-strong army that landed at Ringford, near Dublin, in August of 1649.

The consequences of this Cromwellian conquest still resonate throughout the island today.

Cromwell had three main aims: to quash all forms of rebellion, to 'remove' all Catholic landowners who had taken part in the rebellion, and to convert the native Irish to the Protestant faith.

An early warning of the terrors that were in store for the native Catholic Irish came when the northeastern town of Drogheda was stormed and taken in September and between 2,000 and 4,000 of its inhabitants killed, including priests who were summarily put to the sword.

The defenders of Drogheda's St. Peter's Church, who had also refused to surrender, were burned to death as they huddled for refuge in the steeple and the church was deliberately torched.

It was not long before Cromwell held Ireland in a grip

of iron, allowing him to implement what amounted to a policy of ethnic cleansing.

His troopers were given free rein to hunt down and kill priests, while Catholic estates were confiscated.

Catholic landowners in Ulster, Leinster, and Munster were grudgingly given pathetically small estates west of the river Shannon – where they were hemmed in by colonies of Cromwellian soldiers.

One of the chroniclers of the terrible period of the Cromwellian conquest of Ireland was the poet and scholar Brian Mac Giolla Phádraig, born in the Mac Giolla Phádriag, or Fitzpatrick, homeland of Ossory in 1580.

He was the author of the famous *Faisean Chláir Éibhir*, in which he laments the attempts to destroy Ireland's ancient and proud Gaelic order. He wrote:

A trick of this false world has laid me low: servants in every home with grimy English but no regard for one of the poet class save 'Out! And take your precious Gaelic with you.'

Never a man of arms but simply a scholar and poet, he was nevertheless perceived as a threat to the establishment of Cromwellian order in Ireland.

Appointed vicar general and apostolic vicar of the diocese of Ossory in 1651, he was murdered by Cromwellian troopers about a year later. A memorial to him lies to this day in the village square of Durrow.

One of his important legacies is that, while Cromwell's troops raged throughout Ireland intent on destroying all vestiges of Gaelic culture, he managed to save the precious genealogical and historical work known as the *Book of the O'Byrne*.

Following the devastations that came in the wake of the Cromwellian invasion a further blow to the Gaelic order was struck nearly forty years later in what is known in Ireland as Cogadh an Dá Rí, or The War of the Two Kings.

Also known as the Williamite War in Ireland or the Jacobite War in Ireland, it was sparked off in 1688 when the Stuart monarch James II (James VII of Scotland) was deposed and fled into exile in France.

The Protestant William of Orange and his wife Mary (ironically a daughter of James II) were invited to take up the thrones of Scotland, Ireland, and England – but James still had significant support in Ireland.

His supporters were known as Jacobites, and among them were Fitzpatricks.

Following the arrival in England of William and Mary from Holland, Richard Talbot, 1st Earl of Tyrconnell and James's Lord Deputy in Ireland, assembled an army loyal to the Stuart cause.

The aim was to garrison and fortify the island in the name of James and quell any resistance.

Londonderry, or Derry, proved loyal to the cause of William of Orange, or William III as he had become, and managed to hold out against a siege that was not lifted until July 28, 1689.

James, with the support of troops and money supplied by Louis XIV of France, had landed at Kinsale in March of 1689 and joined forces with his Irish supporters.

A series of military encounters followed, culminating in James's defeat by an army commanded by William at the battle of the Boyne on July 12, 1689.

James fled again into French exile, never to return, while another significant Jacobite defeat occurred in July of 1691 at the battle of Aughrim – with about half their army killed on the field, wounded, or taken prisoner.

The Williamite forces besieged Limerick and the Jacobites were forced into surrender in September of 1691.

A peace treaty, known as the Treaty of Limerick followed, under which those Jacobites willing to swear an oath of loyalty to William were allowed to remain in their native land.

Those reluctant to do so, including many native Irish such as the Fitzpatricks, were allowed to seek exile on foreign shores.

Those who remained managed to adapt to the radically different politics of the time to such an extent that John Fitzpatrick, born in 1719, was later created 1st Earl of Upper Ossory.

Through his marriage in 1744 to Lady Evelyn Leveson-Gower, daughter of the 1st Earl of Gower, his son John Fitzpatrick, 2nd Earl of Upper Ossory, also held the title of Lord Gower.

Both titles became extinct following his death in 1818.

Fitzpatricks, meanwhile, were among the many thousands of Irish who were forced to seek a new life many thousands of miles from their native land during the famine known as The Great Hunger, caused by a failure of the potato crop between 1845 and 1849.

But in many cases Ireland's loss of sons and daughters such as the Fitzpatricks was to the gain of those equally proud nations in which they settled.

Chapter four:
On the world stage

Born in Chicago in 1958 Tony Fitzpatrick is not only an artist whose works grace collections that include New York's Museum of Modern Art, the Art Institute of Chicago, and the Museum of Contemporary Arts in Miami, but who has also had roles in films that include *Philadelphia* and *Primal Fear*.

Back in the Fitzpatrick homeland of Ireland *Jim Fitzpatrick* is the artist renowned for the iconic 1968 two-tone portrait of the revolutionary *Che Guevara*, based on a photograph by Alberto Korda.

Inspired by Ireland's Celtic past, he is also the author and illustrator of a version of the ancient *The Book of Conquests*, while he has also produced artwork for such diverse bands and artistes as Thin Lizzy, Sinéad O'Connor and The Darkness.

In the world of music **Colleen Fitzpatrick**, born in 1969 in Old Bridge, New Jersey, is the American singer, dancer, and actress better known as **Vitamin C**, and whose top-selling singles include *Smile, As Long As You're Loving Me*, and *The Itch*.

In the world of film **James A. Fitzpatrick**, born in 1894 in Shelton, Connecticut, was the American film director, producer, and narrator famed for a series of travel documentaries from the mid 1920s until his death in 1980 that appeared under the titles of 'The Voice of the Globe', and 'Fitzpatrick's Traveltalks.'

On a technical level, **Brad Fitzpatrick**, born 1980 in Iowa, is the American computer programming wizard best known as the creator of several free and highly popular software projects, and who is best known to Internet users as 'bradfitz.'

In the highly competitive sports arena **Sandy Fitzpatrick**, born in 1944 in Paisley, Scotland, is the former professional ice hockey player who played for both the Minnesota North Stars and the New York Rangers, while **Mark Fitzpatrick**, born in 1968 in Toronto, is a former Canadian professional ice hockey goal tender.

Also on the ice **Rory Fitzpatrick**, born in 1975 in Rochester, New York, is the hockey defenceman who, at the time of writing, is with the Vancouver Canucks.

In the swimming pool **Ken Fitzpatrick**, born in 1963 in Ottowa, is the retired Canadian breaststroke swimmer who competed in the 1984 Summer Olympics in Los Angeles, while in the rough and tumble of American football **Ryan Fitzpatrick**, born in 1982 in Gilbert, Arizona is, at the time of writing, a star NFL quarterback for the St. Louis Rams.

On the rugby pitch **Sean Fitzpatrick**, born in 1963 in Auckland, is the internationally acclaimed former New Zealand rugby player better known as 'Fitzy.'

Reckoned to be one of the greatest rugby players New Zealand has ever produced, he captained the All Blacks from 1992 until his retirement from playing in 1997.

On the cricket pitch **Cathyrn Fitzpatrick**, born in 1968 in Melbourne, is the former Australian cricketer who achieved the accolade during her playing career as being one of the world's fastest women pace bowlers.

Now involved in coaching, she was also a member of the Australian team that took the Women's Cricket Cup in both 1997 and 2005.

From cricket to baseball, **John Fitzpatrick**, born in 1904 in LaSalle, Illinois, and who died in 1990, was a noted Major League coach and Minor League manager.

Fitzpatricks have also stamped a mark on the continent of Africa – most notably **Sir James Percy Fitzpatrick**, born in 1862 of Irish parentage in William's Town, South Africa.

His father, **James Coleman Fitzpatrick**, was an influential judge on the Supreme Court of the then Cape Colony, but Fitzpatrick himself was destined for a rather more adventurous career.

Aged in his early twenties he trekked to the Eastern Transvaal goldfields, finding various jobs as a prospector's assistant, storeman, ox-wagon transport rider, and journalist.

An exciting account of his adventurers in Eastern Transvaal was later published as *Jock of the Bushveld*, which remains a bestseller to this day.

Firmly on the side of Britain during the Anglo-Boer War of 1899 to 1902, Fitzpatrick served as official adviser on

South African Affairs to the British government. He was rewarded for his loyalty with the granting of a knighthood at the end of the conflict.

By 1908 he was one of the Transvaal representatives in the National Convention that established the Union of South Africa, later serving as a member of the union's parliament.

Before his death in 1931 he had also established the basis of what is now South Africa's citrus farming industry.

Another titled Fitzpatrick was **Sir Charles Fitzpatrick**, who was born in 1853 in Quebec City and who died in 1942.

A lawyer and politician, he served as Solicitor General for Canada from 1896 to 1902 and later as Minister of Justice.

Back in the Irish Republic two separate Thomas J. Fitzpatricks have served as distinguished politicians. One, born in 1918 in Scotshouse, Clones, Co. Monaghan, was the Fine Gael party politician who held a number of government posts including Minister for Lands from 1973 to 1976 and Minister for Fisheries and Forestry from 1981 to 1982. He died in 2006.

Born in 1926 the other **Thomas J. Fitzpatrick** is the retired Fianna Fáil party politician who was elected no less than six times to the Irish Parliament as the member for Dublin South Central and Dublin Central.

Back in Canada **Brian Fitzpatrick**, born in 1945 in Moose Jaw, Saskatchewan, is the Canadian Alliance Party politician who was first elected to the Canadian House of Commons in 2000, representing the Riding of Prince Albert, and later elected after the Alliance Party merged into the Conservative Party of Canada.

In America **Benjamin Fitzpatrick**, born in 1802 in Greene County, Georgia, was the American lawyer and politician who served as governor of Alabama from 1841 to 1845 and also as a Democrat to the U.S. Senate.

In the world of ecclesiastical affairs **Bishop John Fitzpatrick**, born in 1812 and ordained a priest in 1840 was ordained six years later as the third Catholic Bishop of Boston.

Born in Warrnambool, Victoria, in 1905, **Brian Fitzpatrick** was the noted author, journalist, and historian who was also one of the founders in 1935 of the Australian Council of Civil Liberties, serving as its general secretary from 1939 until his death in 1965.

In the world of medicine **Thomas Fitzpatrick**, born in 1832 in Virginia, Co. Cavan, was the Irish physician who became a member of the distinguished Royal College of Physicians in 1868 while practising in London's famed St. Bartholomew's Hospital. He died in 1900.

In contemporary times the **Fitzpatrick Scale** is named after America's Harvard University dermatologist **T.B. Fitzpatrick** who, in 1975, developed a technique for classifying the response of different types of skin to Ultra-Violet (UV) light.

On the battlefield **Francis Fitzpatrick**, born in 1859 in Tullycorbet, Co. Monaghan, was awarded the Victoria Cross, the highest award for gallantry for British and

Commonwealth forces, while serving with the 94th Regiment during the Basuto War in South Africa.

It was in November of 1879 that Fiztpatrick and another private helped to carry a severely wounded officer to safety while fighting a rearguard action against about 30 of the enemy. He died in his native Ireland in 1933.

Fitzpatricks have also acquired no small degree of notoriety – no less so than **James Fitzpatrick**, better known as the eighteenth century American highwayman **Sandy Flash**.

The son of Irish immigrants to America, the date of his birth is uncertain, but it is thought that he was probably aged in his early twenties when he enlisted in the Continental Army on the outbreak of the Revolutionary War against Britain in 1775.

There then followed a colourful spree as a highwayman, operating west of Philadelphia, Pennsylvania, and gaining a reputation as an eighteenth century Robin Hood.

Finally captured by the exasperated forces of the law he made a number of escape attempts from prison before ultimately facing the hangman's noose in 1778.

One legend is that the bold and wily Sandy Flash buried a glittering pile of loot in what is known as Castle Rock, a hill to the west of Newton township in Delaware County, and near Crum Creek.

The treasure still remains tantalisingly hidden, despite numerous attempts over the years to locate it.

Key dates in Ireland's history from the first settlers to the formation of the Irish Republic:

circa 7000 B.C. Arrival and settlement of Stone Age people.
circa 3000 B.C. Arrival of settlers of New Stone Age period.
circa 600 B.C. First arrival of the Celts.
200 A.D. Establishment of Hill of Tara, Co. Meath, as seat of the High Kings.
circa 432 A.D. Christian mission of St. Patrick.
800-920 A.D. Invasion and subsequent settlement of Vikings.
1002 A.D. Brian Boru recognised as High King.
1014 Brian Boru killed at battle of Clontarf.
1169-1170 Cambro-Norman invasion of the island.
1171 Henry II claims Ireland for the English Crown.
1366 Statutes of Kilkenny ban marriage between native Irish and English.
1529-1536 England's Henry VIII embarks on religious Reformation.
1536 Earl of Kildare rebels against the Crown.
1541 Henry VIII declared King of Ireland.
1558 Accession to English throne of Elizabeth I.
1565 Battle of Affane.
1569-1573 First Desmond Rebellion.
1579-1583 Second Desmond Rebellion.
1594-1603 Nine Years War.
1606 Plantation' of Scottish and English settlers.

1607	Flight of the Earls.
1632-1636	Annals of the Four Masters compiled.
1641	Rebellion over policy of plantation and other grievances.
1649	Beginning of Cromwellian conquest.
1688	Flight into exile in France of Catholic Stuart monarch James II as Protestant Prince William of Orange invited to take throne of England along with his wife, Mary.
1689	William and Mary enthroned as joint monarchs; siege of Derry.
1690	Jacobite forces of James defeated by William at battle of the Boyne (July) and Dublin taken.
1691	Athlone taken by William; Jacobite defeats follow at Aughrim, Galway, and Limerick; conflict ends with Treaty of Limerick (October) and Irish officers allowed to leave for France.
1695	Penal laws introduced to restrict rights of Catholics; banishment of Catholic clergy.
1704	Laws introduced constricting rights of Catholics in landholding and public office.
1728	Franchise removed from Catholics.
1791	Foundation of United Irishmen republican movement.
1796	French invasion force lands in Bantry Bay.
1798	Defeat of Rising in Wexford and death of United Irishmen leaders Wolfe Tone and Lord Edward Fitzgerald.

1800	Act of Union between England and Ireland.
1803	Dublin Rising under Robert Emmet.
1829	Catholics allowed to sit in Parliament.
1845-1849	The Great Hunger: thousands starve to death as potato crop fails and thousands more emigrate.
1856	Phoenix Society founded.
1858	Irish Republican Brotherhood established.
1873	Foundation of Home Rule League.
1893	Foundation of Gaelic League.
1904	Foundation of Irish Reform Association.
1913	Dublin strikes and lockout.
1916	Easter Rising in Dublin and proclamation of an Irish Republic.
1917	Irish Parliament formed after Sinn Fein election victory.
1919-1921	War between Irish Republican Army and British Army.
1922	Irish Free State founded, while six northern counties remain part of United Kingdom as Northern Ireland, or Ulster; civil war up until 1923 between rival republican groups.
1949	Foundation of Irish Republic after all remaining constitutional links with Britain are severed.